PRESERVED RAILWAYS OF EASTERN ENGLAND

Adam Head

AMBERLEY

First published 2020

Amberley Publishing
The Hill, Stroud
Gloucestershire, GL5 4EP

www.amberley-books.com

ISBN 978 1 4456 9738 3 (print)
ISBN 978 1 4456 9739 0 (ebook)

British Library Cataloguing in Publication Data.
A catalogue record for this book is available from the British Library.

Origination by Amberley Publishing.
Printed in the UK.

Contents

Introduction

Around the UK there are 119 preserved railways that occupy various parts of the country. These railways differ from the rest of the UK rail network as they aren't operated by a Train Operated Company (TOC). They are usually set in the period when they were in their heyday, with the most popular being recreated back to the days of steam as it gives the older train enthusiasts memories of days gone by, whilst giving younger train enthusiasts a look into the past before the days of diesels and modern-day units.

In this book, many different preserved railways in the East of England will be visited, ranging from Norfolk and Suffolk to Leicestershire, looking at the home fleet and both steam and diesel locomotives that have visited these railways.

The pictures in this book range between 2012 and 2019. Despite these being preserved railways, the same rules apply to these railways as the UK network itself as these places can be just as dangerous despite their slower running speeds. Some of the images in this book will be slightly lower quality because an older camera was used.

Station	Opened	Closed	Reopened
Barrow Hill Roundhouse	1870	1991	1998
The Bure Valley Railway	1880	1952 (Passenger) 1982 (Freight)	1990
East Anglian Railway Museum	1986		
Epping Ongar Railway	1865	1994	2004
Great Central Railway	1899	1966–69	1974
Managapps Farm Railway	1989		
Mid Norfolk Railway	1847	1964–69 (Passenger) 1989 (Freight)	1995
Nene Valley Railway	1847	1966 (Passenger) 1972 (Freight)	1977
North Norfolk Railway	1887	1964	1975

1

Barrow Hill Roundhouse

Barrow Hill Roundhouse reopened in 1998, after it was closed in 1991 by British Rail. It was saved by the Barrow Hill Engine Shed Society, who wanted to save this building from being demolished and lost forever.

To this day, Barrow Hill Roundhouse still pulls in the crowds and is regularly open to the public. There are a number of locomotives of all kinds on show, as companies such as the Deltic Preservation Society and Harry Needle Railroad Company tend to store their locomotives at this location. For this reason there will always be a need for this roundhouse.

Two different British Rail heavyweights sit inside the roundhouse at Barrow Hill. Seen here are Class 45 Peak 45060 and Class 40s D212 (40012) and D335 (40135). At the time of writing, these three locomotives were in the process of being overhauled.

Barrow Hill is home to unique locomotives, such as this British Rail Class 83 electric locomotive E3035, built between 1960 and 1962. These locomotives spent their lives working on the West Coast Main Line. E3035 (83012) was only one of two of this class to make it into preservation.

Another West Coast Main Line stalwart seen at Barrow Hill is Class 82 electric locomotive E3054 (82008). This locomotive also spent its life working between London Euston and Glasgow Central. Sitting in the sunshine, this is the only member of the entire fleet of ten that made it into preservation.

On 5 November 2016, Class 24 diesel locomotive D5054 (24054) sits at Barrow Hill. This locomotive was in the process of also getting an overhaul and now enjoys life ferrying passengers back and forth on the East Lancashire Railway.

Above and below: Class 20s are regular visitors to Barrow Hill when they are between duties. Despite wearing many different liveries, they are usually hired out to Harry Needle Railroad Company. The spot hire company has many different liveries. 20905 sports GBRf livery, 20314 is in the company's bright orange colours and 20107 is in BR blue.

A unique locomotive that nearly ended up at the scrapyard is 89001, an electric locomotive that spent its life on the East Coast Main Line. It was built by British Rail Engineering Limited (BREL) at Crewe and was the only one of the class ever made. In 1989 it was painted into InterCity Swallow livery and named *Avocet* at London King's Cross. In 1996 it passed over to GNER's hands for use on London King's Cross to Leeds and Bradford services. After a major failure in 2001 it was withdrawn again and was put up for sale in 2006, when it was saved by the AC Locomotive Group, who have since repainted 89001 back into InterCity Executive livery. They are now in the process of giving 89001 a major overhaul. Who knows, maybe it will make a return to the East Coast Main Line?

Class 40 diesel locomotive (D345) 40145 sits at Barrow Hill. Owned by the Class 40 Preservation Group, it entered service in May 1961 and spent most of its life in the North of England, being based at Neville Hill, York and Gateshead depot. It was the first Class 40 to enter preservation in February 1984. As well as wearing its current BR blue livery, it has also worn BR large logo livery and BR Brunswick Green too. In 2002 it obtained a certificate to work on the main line and has since been all over the country.

A scene of times gone by when most depots would have a selection of BR blue locomotives. On the left is a Class 03 diesel shunter. With 230 built between 1957 and 1961, D2066 (03066) is one of fifty-six examples still remaining in preservation. On the right is Class 55 Deltic diesel locomotive 55019, which belongs to the Deltic Preservation Society, who are also based at Barrow Hill. 55019 doesn't have a certificate to run on the main line but that hasn't stopped it visiting various railways, such as the North Norfolk Railway and the Great Central Railway. It attracts many visitors with its distinctive look and sound.

2

The Bure Valley Railway

Stations:
Aylsham
Brampton
Buxton
Coltishall
Wroxham

The entire line was closed in 1982 by British Railway on 6 January and all of the track was pulled up between 1984 and 1985. Despite this, the Bure Valley Railway was reopened in 1990 and still prospers to this very day, celebrating its twenty-fifth anniversary on 10 July 2015 with a gala weekend. The celebrations featured the very first narrow-gauge locomotive on the line and the crew that manned it too. This railway carries around 125,000 passengers each year, with many combining the use of this railway with cruise trips on the Norfolk Broads through the Norfolk Broads National Park.

The closest main line station to alight at for the Bure Valley Railway is Hoveton & Wroxham on the Bittern Line between Norwich and Sheringham. Abellio Greater Anglia provides an hourly service on this line. Class 156 Sprinter 156416 awaits departure from Hoveton & Wroxham with a service for Sheringham.

It isn't always about the trains at preserved railways, as many have attractive signal boxes much like this one seen at Wroxham. It closed on 25 July 2000 after the signalling of the line had been transferred to Trowse Swing Bridge. Since closure it has moved sideways to allow a better line of sight for the drivers heading towards Sheringham on the Bittern Line.

The Bure Valley Railway's stock comprises mostly of steam engines. After arriving from Aylsham, one of their tank engines, 2-6-4 No. 9 *Mark Timothy*, sits at Wroxham after running around its train.

Two narrow gauge tender engines also operate. One of these is 2-6-2 No. 10 *Blickling Hall*, seen here arriving into Coltishall with a service for Wroxham. This locomotive is named after the large Jacobean-style mansion located outside Aylsham.

Another of the tank engines that operates on the Bure Valley Railway is 2-6-2 No. 8 *John of Gaunt*. John of Gaunt was lord of the manor in Aylsham in the fourteenth century and was the son of King Richard III. The locomotive used to be oil fired before it was converted to coal fired in 2005.

Sporting a headboard with the railway's name is 2-6-4 No. 1 *Wroxham Broad* as it arrives into a very warm Buxton with a service for Aylsham. This locomotive was built in 1964 and was due to be sent abroad before staying in the UK and being bought by the Bure Valley Railway in 1991.

A small number of diesel engines operate on the railway. One seen at Aylsham is the 0-4-0 station shunter No. 4. This small shunter is fitted with the engine from a Peugeot 205 diesel car.

One of the diesel locomotives that gets to see more than just Aylsham station is No. 3, named *2nd Air Division USAAF* in memory of the division that operated in the area during the Second World War. It was originally named *Buxton Mill* and is styled on the Class 35 Hymec diesel locomotive.

At the time of writing the locomotive seen in this image is supposed to be 2-6-2 No. 7 *Spitfire* but was in the process of undergoing an overhaul. It was named *Spitfire* after the well-known plane used throughout the Second World War, as many were flown from bases close to the railway.

3

The East Anglian Railway Museum

Hidden away on the Gainsborough line between Marks Tey and Sudbury lies a small station called Chappel & Wakes Colne, which is already well known for its attractive viaduct that has thirty-two arches, is 1,066 feet long and stands 75 feet above the ground.

There is something else at Chappel & Wakes Colne that also draws the passengers in, a hidden gem in the Suffolk countryside: the East Anglian Railway Museum. Located next to the station, on the other side, visitors pay on the side they alight before walking over the footbridge to the museum, which opened in 1986.

The closest main line station to the East Anglian Railway Museum is Chappel & Wakes Colne. The Gainsborough Line is usually operated by Class 153 Sprinters and sometimes Class 156 Sprinters. Abellio Greater Anglia Class 153 Sprinter 153322 sits at Sudbury with a service for Marks Tey whilst displaying a completely different destination.

Before privatisation passed this line over to First Great Eastern, it originally belonged to Network SouthEast and the memory still remains with the station to this day. On the other side is the First Great Eastern sign.

When approaching the East Anglia Railway Museum from the road, visitors will see 0-4-0 saddle tank engine No. 2039, built in 1943 by Peckett & Sons and named *Jeffrey*. This locomotive looks in brilliant condition despite having no protection from the weather.

Andrew Barclay 0-4-0 shunter No. 333 is a resident of the East Anglian Railway Museum and is named *John Peel* after the well-known Radio 1 DJ who lived in Suffolk in a small village called Great Finborough, near Stowmarket.

The East Anglian Railway Museum holds many different railway vehicles not commonly seen by the public, such as this BR 12T diesel rail crane. The railway operates regular demonstration runs with this crane to allow the public to see it in action.

On display and sometimes used are these carriages that were originally used by the Great Eastern Railway. The carriage at the back, No. 553, was a passenger brake van built in 1890, whilst the carriage in front, No. 19, was a first-class carriage built in 1878.

Once a common sight around East Anglia, and the rest of the country, was the Class 101 DMU. This very popular unit was built by Metro-Cammell between 1956 and 1959 and was still in passenger service on the main line right up until 2003. They have all been removed and some have found new lives on preserved railways, such as E56358, which is owned by the Diesel Unit Preservation Associates and still sees regular use.

At the time of visiting the East Anglian Railway Museum in 2016, one of the trains on view was Class 306 electric multiple unit No. 306017. Built by Metro-Cammell and Birmingham Railway Carriage & Wagon Co., it looks very out of place here as it spent its entire life working on the Great Eastern Main Line between London Liverpool Street and Shenfield. No. 306017 has since left the East Anglian Railway Museum and moved to Shildon in County Durham.

Above, below and opposite page: Like many preserved railways, Thomas the Tank Engine days are very common and popular with families. At the East Anglian Railway Museum, they regularly hold these types of events and have trains that look like the characters Toby, with the added bonus of a carriage that looks like his trusty companion Henrietta, as well as Thomas and Percy. The Class 101 DMU is sometimes used as the character Daisy, whose character was based off this unit in the books.

At the end of the platform sits Chappel North signal box, which is painted in the colours of yellow and green, a common sight for signal boxes in the East of England. These were the colours that were chosen by LNER. This signal box, much like Chappel signal box on the other side of the lines, is usually open to visitors to see what life was like for a signalman back in the days of semaphore signalling. Now it controls the points and signals around the yard.

4

The Epping Ongar Railway

Stations:
Epping Forest*
North Weald
Blake Hall**
Ongar

*Epping Forest is a stopping point and has no platforms to allow passengers to alight.
**Blake Hall is a private residence and despite a platform being installed passengers are unable to alight.

A railway that originally started out life as part of the London Underground system is the Epping Ongar Railway, based in Essex, which closed in 1994 and reopened ten years later as a preserved railway.

In the present day this line continues to strive and grow as it hosts multiple events through the year, including steam and diesel train galas, ale trains and Santa specials throughout December. The decision to suspend the line for improvement has paid off a great deal and they can focus on their main goal, which is to connect back to the main network at Epping to allow this branch to become part of London's vast network again.

The Epping Ongar Railway can only be accessed by the London Underground at the tip of the Central Line, after which it is a bus journey to the railway. The line is operated by 1992 stock, which was built by British Rail Engineering Limited (BREL). This 1992 stock departs Epping with a service for West Ruislip. Alternatively, passengers can travel to Shenfield station on the Great Eastern Main Line and get a bus service from there.

Looking rather unloved and abandoned at the end of the line at Ongar is DR73241, which in a past life was a Plasser & Theurer Tamper, being regularly used on engineering possessions. With the track in front missing it may be a while before this moves again.

On 19 September 2015, the Epping Ongar Railway held a diesel gala. One of the visitors to this gala was Class 33 diesel locomotive No. 33202, which was loaned to them from the Mangapps Farm Railway. Here it sits at Ongar waiting for its coaching stock to arrive to form a service for Epping Forest.

Another visitor to the gala in September 2015 was Class 14 shunter No. D9539 from the Ribble Steam Railway and Museum. These shunters are known as 'Teddy Bears' due to the way they were designed. No. D9539 rests up at Ongar having arrived from North Weald.

During their diesel gala in April 2018, the Epping Ongar Railway acquired a pair of Class 20 diesel locomotives, Nos D8059 (20059) and D8001 (20001), both in BR Green. At Ongar, the pair sit side by side after No. D8059 ran round from the front. From the cab of a Class 20 the driver can drive the loco in either direction, unlike other locomotives where the driver would need to walk to the other end.

A locomotive that has lived on the Epping Ongar Railway since 2011 is No. D5557 (31438), which is usually in operation during diesel galas on the railway. D5557 awaits departure from Ongar with a service for Epping Forest. The InterCity blue and grey liveried Mk 2 carriages behind D5557 also compliment the scene.

Class 03 shunter No. D2170 (03170) made an appearance during the April 2018 diesel gala too but was only out on show, as seen here at North Weald.

An unusual visitor during the September 2015 gala was Class 08 shunter No. 08836, wearing GWR green and arriving with No. 205205 in tow. In 2015, First Group rebranded themselves as Great Western Railway in very much the same style as the previous steam operating company during the Big Four days. The following day a GWR company logo was placed on the side of 08836.

Steam engines are also a common sight and they are also maintained at the works at North Weald. On two separate occasions they have been visible from the platform at North Weald station. 0-4-4 tank engine Met 1, built in 1898 and the remaining locomotive of its class, is receiving attention. It spent its life working on the London Underground on the Metropolitan line. In 2015, 2-6-2 No. 4141 was seen at North Weald awaiting its next duty. This locomotive was withdrawn in 1963 and was sent to scrap but fortunately was saved, along with nine more of its classmates. Before withdrawal No. 4141 spent its entire life based at Gloucester helping with banking duties. At the time of writing, 4141 is currently undergoing a major overhaul.

Above and below: One of the many diesel multiple units that resides on the Epping Ongar Railway is No. W56287, which is a Class 121 driving trailer, used with Class 121 'Bubble Cars'. W56287, built in 1961, spent its entire life working on the Great Western Main Line between London Paddington and Oxford. In 2018 it is seen at Ongar waiting to lead a train to Epping Forest. In 2019 it was paired up with their resident Class 117 driving motor standard (DMS) carriage to make a complete DMU, as seen at North Weald.

Another resident of the Epping Ongar Railway is No. D6729 (37029), a Class 37 diesel locomotive that was built in 1961 and allocated to Stratford depot in East London. It was withdrawn in December 1993 and has seen main line work with both private ownership and main line companies, such as Direct Rail Services (DRS), before arriving at its new home in 2010. It is seen here at Ongar after arriving from Epping Forest.

Class 25 diesel locomotive No. D7612 (25262) was kindly loaned to the Epping Ongar Railway from the South Devon Railway for their diesel gala in 2019. These locomotives were known as 'Rats' due to them being seen everywhere around the UK rail network. D7612 waits at Ongar before departing for Epping Forest.

Looking resplendent in its BR large logo livery, Class 47 diesel locomotive No. D1606 (47635) sits at Ongar after arriving from North Weald. The April 2019 diesel gala was the first event for the unveiling of this locomotive after several years out of traffic whilst it was repaired and repainted. 47635 has been a resident at the Epping Ongar Railway after it was withdrawn from traffic by EWS.

A unit that always catches the attention of the crowds is diesel electric multiple unit Class 205 'Thumper' (No. 205205). It is seen here sitting at North Weald in Network SouthEast livery. It is known as a 'Thumper' due to the noise that these units make when they are travelling. It was withdrawn in 2004 by Southern and was put into storage before arriving onto the Epping Ongar Railway in 2009. 205205 was built with a corridor connection making it unique as it was the only member of the class to have this installed.

5

The Great Central Railway

Stations:
Loughborough Central
Quorn & Woodhouse
Rothley
Leicester North

Based in Leicestershire, there is a very popular, unique preserved railway called the Great Central Railway. The reason this railway is unusual, compared to the others in this book, is because it used to be part of a main line that ran through the Midlands into London called the Great Central Main Line (aka the London Extension), which ran from Sheffield through Nottingham and towards London Marylebone.

The Great Central Railway has to be one of the biggest railway successes to rise from the ashes of the Beeching Axe, which closed the line between 1966 and 1969 and will continue to live on for many generations to come.

Above left and right: The closest main line station for the Great Central Railway is Loughborough, which is a short walk away from the station. The only operator that serves this station is East Midlands Railway. Class 222 Meridian No. 222103 sits at Loughborough with a service for Sheffield. A local service between Leicester and Lincoln also stops at this station, as seen with Class 156 Sprinter No. 156410 with a service for Leicester.

The Great Central Railway run dining services throughout the entire year, the concept being that food is delivered to your seat whilst the train passes through the countryside. Special dining carriages are used for these services and a steam engine usually hauls the train. In March 2017, LMS 2-6-0 Class 2 No. 46521 sits at Loughborough Central awaiting departure for Leicester North.

Steam engines play a large part in the operations at the Great Central Railway. In August 2018 the railway recreated the final days of British Railway steam as it was the fiftieth anniversary of British Rail pulling the plug on steam-operated trains on the UK rail network in 1968. A multitude of locomotives were used, including British Railways Standard 2MT 2-6-0 locomotive No. 78018, which is seen pulling out of Loughborough Central yard to form a service for Leicester North.

Looking more like a scene from 1967, rather than 2017, resident Class 101 diesel multiple unit carriage No. 51427 and LMS 2-6-0 Class 2 No. 46521 are both seen at Loughborough Central awaiting their next duties.

Loughborough Central sits a short walk from the yard and steam workshop. Visitors are allowed access to this when visiting the railway. There is usually a large variety of engines on view to the public, such as LMS Black Five 4-6-0. No. 45305, Southern Railway King Arthur Class 4-6-0 No. 30777, and Great Northern Railway Class N2 0-6-2 No. 1744, which are seen in 2016. Both 45305 and 30777 are residents of the railway, whereas 1744 was only a visitor and left the railway a month later.

The railway's resident diesel locomotives are also stabled in the yard when they aren't in use. One of the many resident locomotives is Class 45 Peak No. D123 (45125), which is seen awaiting its next duty.

Seen after shunting stock into Loughborough Central yard is Class 47 diesel locomotive No. D1705 (47117). This locomotive was built locally at Loughborough Brush works in 1965 and arrived onto the Great Central Railway in 1996. In 2018 it was unveiled in BR Blue livery with the nameplate *Sparrowhawk* after spending many years in BR two-tone green livery.

The Travelling Post Office (TPO) can also be seen on the Great Central Railway as the railway owns a large number of former Post Office carriages. Some are also based on the Nene Valley Railway. These used to travel across the UK rail network at night before its demise in 2004. No. D123 leaves Loughborough yard with a TPO demonstration run.

A visitor to the railway's diesel gala in 2017 was Class 33 diesel locomotive No. 33063, which was loaned to the railway from the Spa Valley Railway in East Sussex. The locomotive wears Mainline livery and is named *R. J. Mitchell Designer of the Spitfire* after the well-known plane used during the Second World War. It is seen here at Loughborough Central waiting for its next duty.

Above and below: During the March 2017 diesel gala visitors were able to travel behind locos that aren't regularly seen in passenger service, such as Class 08 shunters. The Great Central Railway hired No. 08480 from Railway Support Services to work alongside two of their resident shunters, No. 08694 in EWS livery and No. 08907 in DB livery. The shunters are seen at Loughborough Central before travelling very slowly to Quorn & Woodhouse at a maximum speed of 15 mph – it wasn't a high-speed service!

No. 08907 was also used during the 'End of BR Steam' event, in August 2018, to shunt stock out of Loughborough Central when it wasn't needed. Since this image was taken, 08907 has been repainted from its DB livery to BR green.

A locomotive that has had quite a past is resident Class 37 No. 37714, which is seen at Loughborough Central showing off its new livery of BR Railfreight grey (Metals Sector) in 2017. It previously wore Direct Rail Services livery, albeit without the well-known compass logo, as it was a shunter at Daventry before it arrived at the Great Central Railway. Seen at Leicester North in 2016, this locomotive was built in 1961 with the number D6724 and has seen work aboard and with EWS.

The platforms at Leicester North provide enthusiasts with a good vantage point for when locomotives are being uncoupled from their trains in preparation for them to run around back to Loughborough Central. In September 2016 the railway paid host to Class 55 Deltic No. 55019.

Class 31 diesel locomotives are popular with enthusiasts, especially when the opportunity to see a Network Rail one arises. Seen here at Leicester North, 31105 was a visitor in September 2016. This loco now lives on the Mangapps Farm Railway in Essex. D5830, in experimental ochre livery, is also seen at Leicester North having arrived from Loughborough Central. This locomotive now resides at the Great Central North Railway at Ruddington.

Above and below: Among its large diesel locomotive collection is Class 25 diesel locomotive D5185 (25035). This locomotive arrived at the Great Central Railway in 2002, after a great deal of work was needed to the bodywork. Since then it has been a hard worker for the Great Central Railway and is seen in regular use. In September 2019 it gained a classmate to play with in the form of D7535, which was leant to the Great Central Railway from the South Devon Railway. The locomotives worked together in multiple to Leicester North before being uncoupled to run around its train.

A locomotive that caused an uproar in 2019 is Class 50 diesel locomotive 50017. This locomotive entered service in 1968 and was designed to work on the Great Western Main Line in and out of London Paddington. It went up for sale at the beginning of 2019 but no buyers were found and it was thought it was destined for the scrapyard until the Great Central Railway bought it. Currently it wears Network SouthEast livery but with a new life on this railway it could all change.

D1705 arrives into Quorn & Woodhouse with a service for Leicester North.

Another TPO demonstration run is seen passing through Quorn & Woodhouse. This train came in behind another visitor to the Great Central Railway in 2019, which was Class 42 Warship D821, also present at the September 2019 diesel gala. The Class 42 hydraulics were also found on the Great Western Main Line during the 1960s until they were retired at the end of the decade and the early 1970s. Sadly only two made it to preservation despite thirty-eight being built.

Another resident diesel locomotive is Class 27 D5401, seen here at Rothley with a service for Loughborough Central. This locomotive arrived onto the Great Central Railway in 1994 before departing and coming back again. It spent a lot of its life working in Scotland on push-pull services and other duties. They were built between 1961 and 1962.

A special treat for visitors who attended the diesel gala in September 2019 was this carriage parked at Quorn & Woodhouse. It originally belonged to the Derby Technical Centre and was known at Test Car 2 or ADB 975397. It wears the original livery it gained when it used to work for British Railway. This carriage was used for slip/brake testing of wagons on the West Coast Main Line and, as a result of some of the testing that this carriage did, it now plays a part in some of the air-braked high-speed freight runs on the network today.

6

Mangapps Railway Museum

Stations:
Mangapps
Old Heath*

*The buildings at Old Heath station were originally Laxfield station on the Mid-Suffolk Light Railway before it closed in 1952.

A railway museum hidden away in Burnham-on-Crouch, Essex, is the Mangapps Railway Museum, which may not have the longest running line at 0.75 miles, but still provides a great day out especially with the large amount of interactive railwayana, which opened in 1989.

The museum boasts a large number of signs from many different areas of the UK rail network, from many different eras, both privatised and nationalised, whilst understandably a large amount of it is from the Eastern region of the network. There is also an interactive signalling area where visitors can try their hand at being a signaller and pulling the levers that make semaphore signals move.

The Mangapps Railway Museum provides plenty to keep everyone occupied.

One of main features at the Mangapps Farm Railway is this Canadian Pacific caboose, which was transported from America and now provides trips up and down the railway. The caboose has an upper seating section, as seen in the middle, to give passengers a view over the railway.

Mangapps owns a number of different trains from many different areas of the country. 1954 0-4-0 diesel shunter No. 1 *Elland* was originally a shunter for Elland Power Station in West Yorkshire. After this power plant was decommissioned in 1991, the shunter found new life on this railway.

The railway boasts a lot of static exhibitions at the museum such as 0-6-0 saddle tank No. 358 *Minnie*. It was only one of three locomotives of their type to be built in the UK in 1878 and was preserved in 1968.

Above: One half of a Class 117 diesel multiple unit operates. No. 51381, as seen at Mangapps, waits for a locomotive to haul it to Old Heath rather than Wickford.

Opposite page below and this page: Of the 230 Class 03 diesel shunters that were built, four of them have found themselves living on the Mangapps Farm Railway. Three of these are Nos 03081, which is seen at Mangapps with a brake van special from Old Heath; 03197, which is seen departing Mangapps for Old Heath; and 03089, which awaits departure with the Canadian Pacific caboose.

A single Class 04 shunter also lives on this railway. D2325, built in 1961, was, at one point, based at Norwich like No. 03089. Seen arriving into Mangapps, it has since received a new coat of paint and a plaque on the side commemorating thirty years of the Mangapps Farm Railway opening.

In August 2016, the railway had a diesel gala with all of their diesel locomotives in operation on the day. One of these was this visitor, 0-4-0 diesel shunter AD226, arriving into Mangapps before forming a service for Old Heath.

Above and below: The museum prides itself on its large amount of railwayana from the Eastern region of the UK rail network. Many different signs hang from many different operators from both the nationalised and privatised eras.

Used more as a vantage point for enthusiasts than as a signal box, Mangapps Junction box wears the colours of LNER as Essex was one of the Eastern areas that they operated during the Big Four days.

One of the trains owned by the Mangapps has a claim to fame: this former London Underground Northern Line driving carriage, No. 1030, built by Metro-Cammell in 1959. It was used in the film *The Darkest Hour* in 2017.

Above and below: Loaned steam engines could be regularly seen at the Mangapps Farm Railway during their bank holiday event in August 2019. Two locomotives that were seen were Hawthorn Leslie 0-4-0 saddle tank *Achilles* and British Railways Standard Class 4 2-6-4 No. 80078. The latter was shortly prepared for the next day.

A former London, Tilbury & Southend Railway Class 302 electric multiple unit lives on the Mangapps Farm Railway. Originally built in 1958, they spent their lives working London Fenchurch Street to Southend, as well as services from London Liverpool Street towards Shenfield. They were all withdrawn by 1999. No. 302201 was the only unit of the fleet to survive into preservation.

During the August 2016 diesel gala, the Mangapps Farm Railway's Class 47 diesel locomotive No. 47579, as part of its home fleet, was in operation. With Class 31 diesel locomotive No. 31430 in tow, the train approaches a scene from the BR blue era, arriving into Mangapps.

In 2019, during the bank holiday in August, the railway hosted a steam/diesel open day, with diesel trains in operation on the first day and steam on the second. The railway has large photograph areas for enthusiasts. Class 03 shunter No. 03197 and Class 33 diesel locomotive No. 33202 bask in the sunshine, whilst No. 47579 departs for Old Heath.

In 2018, after several years working for Network Rail, two Class 31s were delivered to the Mangapps Farm Railway. Both of these were in operation during the August bank holiday event in 2019. No. 31105 sits in the yard awaiting its next duty.

Another Class 31 that Mangapps received delivery of was No. 31233 (right). Here it is seen with sister class member No. 31105 (left) with No. 33202 (middle), which also came back to Mangapps Farm Railway for this event.

Utilising No. 302201 as coaching stock, both Nos 31233 and 31105 worked together during the weekend bringing in large crowds of people who may have never been behind a former Network Rail locomotive. Like many other older diesel locomotives, they are known for their loud noise and didn't disappoint as it departed Mangapps for Old Heath.

Above and below: Another loco for the August bank holiday weekend was Class 33 diesel locomotive No. 33202, seen sitting in the yard at Mangapps, awaiting its turn to run down to Old Heath. 33202 is seen later with Nos 302201 and 31105. Built in 1962 in Birmingham, it operated until the late 1980s before being withdrawn and sold to Mangapps.

Above and below: Looking immaculate in its BR large logo livery in the yard is No. 47579. It too is waiting for its turn for the run to Old Heath, which, much like No. 33202, it did with the help of Nos 302201 and 31105. Built in 1964 as No. D1778, before becoming No. 47183 in 1974 and No. 47793 in 1995, it has seen a lot of work, being based at Stratford, Leeds and Immingham depots in its lifetime. It was withdrawn in 2004 and moved to the Mangapps Farm Railway a few years later.

7

The Mid-Norfolk Railway

Stations:
Wymondham Abbey
Kimberley Park
Hardingham*
Thuxton
Yaxham
Dereham

*Hardingham is a private station and is not open to the public.

One area badly affected by the Beeching cuts was East Anglia with many branch lines across the entire region being closed. One of these lines was the Wymondham–Fakenham branch in Norfolk.

In 1964, the section of the line between Dereham and Wells had been closed, with the line being reduced to single track between Wymondham and Dereham. In 1965, and three years later in September 1968, passenger services from King's Lynn were stopped, with services between Wymondham and Dereham following a year later. Freight trains stopped running on this line in 1989, thus completely closing this line. Six years in 1995 the Mid-Norfolk Railway Preservation Trust (MNRPT) was formed.

The railway has grown significantly since 1999 as it continues to rebuild what once stood. With 15 miles of track in use, it is one of longest preserved railways not only in East Anglia but in the UK.

The closest main line station to Wymondham Abbey is Wymondham, on the Breckland Line between Norwich and Ely. It is served by an hourly Abellio Greater Anglia with Class 170 Turbostars. No. 170204 arrives into Wymondham with a service for Cambridge.

Above and below: During the summer months, the Mid-Norfolk Railway hire in a steam locomotive to operate services back and forth along the line alongside one of the home diesel locomotives. In 2016 it was the turn of Great Western Railway 0-6-0 Pannier Tank No. 9466, seen arriving into Wymondham Abbey. In 2017 it was the turn of British Railways Standard Class 4 2-6-4 No. 80078, which pulls into the loop at Wymondham Abbey. The railway doesn't have a turntable so all steam engines must run around their trains at the end of the line.

In April 2016 the Mid-Norfolk Railway got a special visitor for the diesel gala in the form of No. 41001, the prototype HST from the 125 Group. This prototype formed the base for the InterCity 125 high-speed train, still seen in operation on the UK network today. The two differences between 41001 and the other HST power cars are, firstly, the design, as Sir Kenneth Grange completely redesigned it, giving its iconic look, and, secondly, the engine, as it has an original Valenta, whereas all other power cars operated by Arriva CrossCountry and LNER use an MTU engine. This special visitor brought in a large number of people.

Freight operator GBRf are well known for lending preserved railways their locos. For preserved railways in East Anglia, GBRf's depot is based in Peterborough so it isn't too far away to get a loco. On a chilly December's day in 2016, GBRf lent the Mid-Norfolk Railway Class 66 diesel locomotive No. 66776, which for some people was interesting due to the rarity of a 66 on a passenger service. The Mid-Norfolk Railway usually put an event on between Christmas and New Year.

The Mid-Norfolk Railway boasts many different lineside positions for enthusiasts trying to get a different type of image that doesn't involve a station. In May 2016, the Mid-Norfolk Railway hosted a Stratford depot event in which one of their home diesel locomotives, Class 47 No. 47596, was temporarily changed to No. 47581. The lineside location seen here is Crownthorpe, which is a small village outside Wymondham where the railway line crosses over the road.

Class 47 diesel locomotive No. 47596 is seen earlier in the day at Thuxton station, awaiting departure for Wymondham Abbey.

One of the visitors to the September 2016 diesel gala was Class 46 Peak No. D182 (46045), which is one of three of this fifty-six-member class that was saved from the cutter's torch. It is based at the Midland Centre in Butterley, in Derbyshire. The summer sun shows off its British Rail blue as it waits for departure for Wymondham Abbey.

A year after GBRf had lent the Mid-Norfolk Railway a Class 66, they did it again with No. 66763, as seen here at Thuxton hauling No. 47596 and a mixed rake of carriages in InterCity, Virgin and Anglia Railways liveries. Seven months previous, No. 66763 received its Severn Valley Railway nameplates, making it the second GBRf 66 to receive preserved railway nameplates after No. 66757 was named *West Somerset Railway* in 2015.

Above and below: Direct Rail Services (DRS) are also known for the lending of locomotives to preserved railways. This is usually due to them having a number of locos stabled at Norwich station when not in use. In April 2016, DRS lent the Mid-Norfolk Railway Class 66 diesel locomotive No. 66426 in its all-over blue livery. A year later, DRS lent the Mid-Norfolk Railway Class 37 diesel locomotive No. 37424 (37558). This locomotive was the first of many to be repainted into BR large logo livery, attracting a lot of visitors to the railway. It was unveiled in this livery with the nameplates *Avro Vulcan XH558* at the DRS open day in July 2016.

Above and below: A Class 37 diesel locomotive was not an uncommon sight at the Mid-Norfolk Railway. For several years the railway owned a Class 37 as part of their home fleet. No. 37003 is seen at Thuxton in 2013 with a service for Wymondham Abbey. At the time of writing, this locomotive is currently receiving an overhaul at Leicester after being out of service for several years. Another DRS hire that was also seen in 2013 as a visitor to the railway's diesel gala, but has unfortunately been scrapped since this picture was taken, was No. 37194.

A very unique and special visitor to the railway's end of year event in 2014 was the brand-new Direct Rail Service (DRS) Class 68 diesel locomotive No. 68007. Built in 2013 in Spain, and delivered to the UK in 2014, it hadn't been in the country a year before passengers were able to travel behind this brand-new locomotive. The opinion was good, and these locomotives have now gone onto be well liked by enthusiasts. 68007 has now moved to Scotland to work for Abellio Scotrail.

A pair of Class 20 diesel locomotives, Nos D8188 and D8059, were also visitors alongside D182 in the railway's diesel gala in September 2016. They are seen working together on the rear of a train at Thuxton waiting for departure for Dereham.

Proving not to be overshadowed by No. 41001, Class 50 diesel locomotive No. 50017 also made an appearance in the April 2016 diesel gala. Seen showing off its immaculate Network SouthEast livery, it awaits departure from Thuxton with a service for Wymondham Abbey.

A long-term former visitor to the Mid-Norfolk Railway was Class 45 Peak No. 45133. This spent several years at the Mid-Norfolk Railway performing at many different events and galas. It has now since left as it receives an overhaul at the Midland Railway Centre in Butterley.

An unusual idea for an event in November 2012 was an event based solely on diesel multiple units. This idea saw their home fleet of DMUs operating, as well as this visitor from East Midlands Trains in the form of Class 158 Sprinter No. 158770, seen arriving into Thuxton.

The Mid-Norfolk Railway was also the home of Southern based 3CIG unit No. 1497. It received this unit in 2010 after it was withdrawn by South West Trains. It was also seen working with a unit due to it being a third rail unit. It is seen at Thuxton with No. 73210 with a service for Wymondham Abbey. 1497 has since left the Mid-Norfolk Railway and now resides on the Spa Valley Railway.

Network SouthEast Class 08 shunter No. 08631 sits at Dereham with a local service. This shunter has since left the railway, moving to Crewe, and has lost its NSE livery in favour of all-over BR blue. Back in 2013, though, passengers were able to travel behind it and see how fast depot shunters go every day.

Looking for a little TLC, Class 73 diesel-electric locomotive No. 73210 sits in Dereham yard. This loco was originally part of the home fleet on this railway and was regularly paired up with the 3CIG No. 1497. It has since left the railway and now lives on the Ecclesbourne Valley Railway in Derbyshire. This loco is named Selhurst after the Southern depot in Croydon.

There weren't two but four Class 20s at the September 2016 diesel gala, with the addition of Nos 20189 and 20205. Unfortunately, on the Saturday they weren't in operation and instead took a long rest in the yard at Dereham.

Above and below: In September 2015, the Mid-Norfolk Railway hired a pair of Class 20s from the Harry Needle Railroad Company. In their striking, bright orange livery, Nos 20311 and 20314 are seen at Dereham running around their train before awaiting departure from the station with a service back to Wymondham Abbey.

To finish the line-up for the September 2016 diesel gala was Class 35 Hymek No. D7017. These diesel hydraulic locos were built between 1961 and 1964 for the Western region. D7017 is based at the West Somerset Railway and is only one of four (alongside D7018, D7029 and D7076) from 101 built that made it into preservation. An unusual visitor to the Eastern region, D7017 is slowly drawn forward to its stock to form a service for Wymondham Abbey.

In September 2012 the Class 47 diesel locomotive celebrated fifty years of service in the UK and, as a result, the Mid-Norfolk Railway hosted a Class 47 gala with the running of eight Class 47s. Sporting a fifty years headboard, seen at Dereham, is No. 47401 *North Eastern*. Built No. D1500 in 1962, it was the very first Class 47 to roll off the production line at Brush Falcon Works. On this day it celebrated fifty years with Nos 47292, 47375, 47579, 47580, 47703, 47798 and 47853.

Another year, another GBRf Class 66. This time, in March 2015, the railway was lent No. 66733 *Cambridge PSB* from GBRf for their spring diesel gala. It is seen, as the sun goes down at Dereham, with a service for Wymondham Abbey.

To start the new year off the Mid-Norfolk Railway hosted an event in January 2016 with a visitor in the form of Direct Rail Service Class 57 diesel locomotive No. 57306. This locomotive had recently been working the East Anglian Railhead Treatment Train circuit (RHTT) and had yet to receive a wash as can be seen by the muck all down the body. In a past life, 57306 was originally No. 47814 before conversion in 2003.

Class 55 Deltic No. 55022 was a visitor to the railway in March 2012, alongside Class 40 No. D335, as an English theme was being applied. 55022 sits at Dereham between duties.

The railway hosted a Stratford depot event in May 2012, with a special visitor from DRS also making an appearance in the form of work-worn Class 37 diesel locomotive No. 37087, which at one point was allocated to the East London depot. No. 37087 ran services back and forth between Wymondham Abbey and Dereham all day before going back to Norwich the same day. Sadly, this locomotive has also been scrapped despite attempts to get it preserved.

Former DRS Class 37 No. 37688 found a new home at the Mid-Norfolk Railway in 2017, providing enthusiasts the opportunity to travel behind the newest member of their home fleet, which was out for all diesel events during 2017. Seen at Dereham with DRS compass logo remains still visible on the bodyside, 37688 runs around its train in preparation to form a service for Wymondham Abbey. In 2018 it moved to the Severn Valley Railway.

Another member of the Mid-Norfolk Railway's home fleet, seen in 2014, is Class 31 diesel locomotive No. 31235. Seen passing through Dereham after arriving from Wymondham Abbey, it arrived onto the railway in 2000 and gave several years of service before suffering a major failure in 2014. The locomotive was sold in 2016 and has moved to the Dean Forest Railway in Gloucestershire.

No. 45133 awaits its coaching stock at Dereham before forming a service for Wymondham Abbey. The opposite platform/running line provides a brilliant spot for enthusiasts to get a picture of locos.

Part of the Stratford 47 group's fleet is No. 47367. This is one of three 47s that they own, the others being Nos 47580 *County of Essex* and 47596 *Aldeburgh Festival*. Nos 47367 and 47596 are only able to operate on preserved railways due to the lack of required equipment and a main line operating license. In 2014, 47367 was moved from the North Norfolk Railway to the Mid-Norfolk Railway where it still resides to this day.

The Mid-Norfolk Railway has hosted many well-known steam engines over the years. In June 2016, for their steam gala, they had two visitors in the form of LMS Princess Coronation Class 4-6-2 No. 46233 *Duchess of Sutherland* and LMS Royal Scot Class 4-6-0 No. 46100 *Royal Scot*, which is seen idling at Dereham.

8

The Nene Valley Railway

Stations:
Peterborough Nene Valley
Orton Mere
Overton for Ferry Meadows
Wansford
Yarwell

On the East Coast Main Line, at Peterborough, is the Nene Valley Railway, based at Wansford, where an entirely volunteer-based group of people work hard to keep a 7.5-mile single track preserved line running. The line goes to Peterborough via Orton Mere and opened in 1977, with the extension to Peterborough from Wansford opening in 1986.

The line was also a victim of the Beeching Axe as less and less passengers used this line in favour of the car. Therefore, the withdrawal of passenger services between Northampton Bridge Street and Peterborough North occurred in July 1963. Despite many lines being closed around the country, this was met with opposition. However, it wasn't enough as the line was closed to passenger services in May 1964, although iron ore freight trains continued to run until 1966. British Railways withdrew all freight by 1972.

Every year the Nene Valley is open near enough all year round and has a variety of different events that feature both steam and diesel locomotives. There is something for everyone at the Nene Valley Railway, which can be accessed by road from either end of the railway or is a short walk away from Peterborough station itself.

The closest main line station for the Nene Valley Railway is Peterborough on the East Coast Main Line. The main operator for this station is LNER, who provide services to and from London King's Cross using Class 91 loco hauled sets. Seen wearing a special InterCity Swallow livery, No. 91119 departs Peterborough with a service for London King's Cross.

DB have been known to lend their locos to the Nene Valley Railway as they too have a depot based in Peterborough alongside GBRf. In April 2015, for their diesel gala, the railway borrowed No. 60001 from DB. Built between 1989 and 1993 by Brush, 100 of these locomotives were built and all were passed over to EWS at the start of privatisation. Luckily, 60001 still sees regular use, whereas many are now seen stored at Toton.

In April 2018, a pair of Class 20s were brought in for their diesel gala in contrasting liveries. Leading the pair is No. 20142 *Sir John Betjeman*, wearing a special London Transport livery to celebrate 150 years of the London Underground, whilst trailing on the rear is No. 20007 in all-over BR green.

The Class 31 diesel locomotive celebrated fifty years of operation in 2017 and to celebrate the Nene Valley Railway hosted a fiftieth anniversary gala event in October. Eight visitors were used for this event, with one of them being No. 31466, seen at Peterborough Nene Valley still wearing the livery of its old operator. This loco was lent to the Nene Valley Railway from the Dean Valley Railway.

An unusual view of No. 47765 as it sits in Wansford yard wearing its undercoat, as there wasn't enough time to have it painted before its appearance at the Nene Valley Railway in 2012. It now wears Scotrail livery and visited the Nene Valley Railway again two years later.

Above and below: For their October 2013 diesel gala, No. 56301 visited the Nene Valley Railway. These locomotives are known more for their freight operations rather than passenger services. 56301 was still wearing the colours of Fastline, who had gone bust three years earlier and had now passed over into preservation to Class 56 Group. It hasn't been the only Class 56 to visit the Nene Valley Railway, though, as No. 56312, advertising the Railfest at the National Railway Museum, visited the Nene Valley Railway in May 2012.

A visitor that unfortunately wasn't part of the event was Rail Operations Group (ROG). Class 47 diesel locomotive No. 47813 had brought the convoy of locos down to the railway for their diesel gala in April 2018 but was only on show for the entire weekend in Wansford yard.

A long-term visitor to the Nene Valley Railway was A1A-owned Class 31 diesel locomotive No. 31271. This replaced No. 31108, which had seen residence for several years. It wears BR sector construction livery and *Stratford 1840–2001* nameplates in memory of the former Eastern region depot. This loco has since left the Nene Valley Railway and now spends its time on the Llangollen Railway in Wales.

There were eight visitors to the Class 31 fiftieth anniversary gala event in October 2017. When they weren't in use, they were parked at Wansford yard for enthusiasts to view. Visible in Wansford yard were Nos 31285, 31452, 31459, 31271, 31108 and 31465, all showing off their various different liveries and designs.

Above and below: The railway also owns two Class 14 shunters as part of their home fleet. Both of these 'Teddy Bears' are regular performers on the railways, operating services between Wansford and Yarwell Junction, or for D9520, a service for Peterborough Nene Valley. Their other Class 14, No. D9529, is seen in Wansford yard awaiting its next duty. This was out for the railway's diesel gala in October 2019.

Resting between duties in Wansford yard during the Nene Valley Railway's diesel gala in April 2018 was No. D182, which was a visitor to this event.

The footbridge at Wansford station provides a great vantage point for trains entering, leaving and shunting around the yard. Located next to the station, during the October 2019 diesel gala visitors were able to watch *Flying Scotsman* being fired and prepared for departure, as this was due to leave the railway the following day for the National Railway Museum in York. To the left is Class 45 Peak No. 45041, which arrived at the Nene Valley Railway after it left the Great Central Railway in 2016 and has resided there ever since.

Above and opposite page: Three visitors to the railway's diesel gala in October 2019 came in the form of Class 37 diesel locomotive No. 37109, which is a resident of the East Lancashire Railway in Lancashire, Class 17 Clayton No. D8568 and Deltic Preservation Group's Class 55 Deltic No. 55019 *Royal Highland Fusilier*. All three of these locos brought in a large number of visitors to the railway as they are all seen at different points of the day at Wansford.

RS68
D8568
55 019
WORKING LOAD 140 TONS
RANSOMES & RAPIER Ltd
IPSWICH 1930 ENGLAND

GBRf have also lent their Class 66s to the Nene Valley Railway as they have a depot located outside Peterborough station, so their locos don't have too far to travel before reaching the railway. In April 2018, with a new number and new livery, No. 66781 sits on the turntable at Wansford awaiting its next duty. This 66 was originally No. 66016 and was built for EWS, then DB before being sold to GBRf in 2018.

The Nene Valley Railway is known for being a railway that runs stock that used to operate in Europe and this unique Swedish railcar makes for a different journey on the railway. The railcar is a Y7 series railcar built by Statens Järnvägar in Sweden, and was in service until the late 1980s. In 1985, the Nene Valley Railway took delivery of No. 1212 *Helga* and it has now been restored to working order, ferrying passengers up and down the line. It is seen in operation in October 2016 at Yarwell Junction awaiting departure for Wansford.

9

The North Norfolk Railway

Stations:
Sheringham
Weybourne
Kelling Heath Park
Holt

Another East Anglian victim of the Beeching Axe was the North Norfolk Railway, located on the Norfolk coast between Sheringham and Holt. This line provides stunning views of the Norfolk coastline, and what it lacks in length it makes up for with the view.

The M&GNJR were known for building railway lines in sparse areas such as the countryside. This would later become their downfall as BR was starting to cut back on lines that weren't profitable. This was mainly due to road transport becoming much more popular and cheaper to operate after the Second World War, and by 1958, British Railways decided that most of the M&GNJR network was to be closed. By February 1959 it had closed.

By July 1975 the line was reopened between Sheringham and Weybourne and by March 1989, having spent their weekends clearing away the undergrowth and vegetation that had grown over the years, as well as relaying the track, the section to Holt station was opened.

Over the past decade the railway has seen an increase in facilities through donations from visitors and from Heritage Lottery funding. The funding has seen the purchasing and restoration of Sheringham station as well as maintenance sheds outside Holt station, which allows their rolling stock to be protected from the elements, as well as receiving restoration work on site, rather than having to send it away to other railways to be completed. Since then the North Norfolk Railway has become a tale of a company that started with very little and have gone on to become a very successful railway.

The closest main line station for the North Norfolk Railway is Sheringham, which is the terminus station on the Bittern Line between Norwich and Sheringham. Abellio Greater Anglia operate this line with Class 153 and Class 156 Sprinters, or sometimes Class 170 Turbostars, as seen here as No. 170208 awaits departure for Norwich.

Sheringham station is where journeys begin on the North Norfolk Railway and it has been lovingly restored over the years with the addition of a footbridge in 2016. One of the railway's home fleet locomotives is Class 37 diesel locomotive No. D6732 (37032), which was built in 1962 and has spent many years at the North Norfolk Railway.

The North Norfolk Railway hosts both diesel and steam engine days. In May 2018, British Rail Standard Class 4 2-6-0 No. 76084 is seen at Sheringham running around its train before heading for Holt.

A colourful visitor to the railway's June 2016 diesel gala event was Class 20 diesel locomotive No. 20227, which was wearing a special livery celebrating 150 years of the London Underground. It is seen at Sheringham awaiting its next duty. No. 20227 has since been repainted into London Transport metropolitan livery and is now named *Sherlock Holmes* after the fictional detective.

Direct Rail Services lent the North Norfolk Railway Class 37 diesel locomotive No. 37605 for their diesel gala event in June 2017. Making its presence known at Sheringham, as it was working with another English Electric stalwart in the form of No. 20227, it waits to run around its train.

Also present for the June 2017 diesel gala was Class 44 Peak D8, which came from Peak Rail in Derbyshire. Of the ten trains built, D8 was only one of two that survived into preservation, with the other being D4. Looking smart in its BR green livery, it sits at Sheringham having arrived from Holt.

Class 33 diesel locomotive No. 33035 was one of the visitors that came to the North Norfolk Railway for their yearly diesel gala in June 2016. Borrowed from the Ecclesbourne Valley Railway in Derbyshire, it awaits departure for Holt in the summer sunshine.

A rare visitor to the Eastern region was Class 56 Group's No. 56301, which was built in Doncaster in 1978 as No. 56045 before gaining its new number in 2006. It was placed into storage in 2010, after Fastline went bust, and was bought by the Class 56 Group in the same year. It still sees regular use mainly in the Leicester area.

Another visitor to the June 2016 diesel gala was No. 50026, which had only been repainted into Network SouthEast livery. It was seen showing off its new paint scheme to the enthusiasts at Sheringham before forming a train to Holt. During this event, the railway was also celebrating thirty years of Network SouthEast, as it started operating in June 1986, and as such locos throughout the day wore a headboard celebrating thirty years of Network SouthEast.

One of the railway's home fleet is LNER 4-6-0 B12 No. 8572, wearing a very striking apple green livery. When locomotives aren't being used, they are usually parked in the yard at Weybourne, which is next to Weybourne station and can be viewed from the platforms. 8572 is seen in Weybourne yard between duties.

British Railways Class 9F 2-10-0 No. 92203 *Black Prince* is another member of the steam home fleet on the North Norfolk Railway. It is seen arriving into Weybourne with a service for Holt in May 2018. These large locomotives were the last steam locomotives to be built by British Railway and were mainly designed to haul freight trains, although they could be seen hauling passenger services from time to time.

In June 2018, rather than having their usual yearly diesel gala they decided to try something different in the form of a mixed traction gala, which saw the railway operating both steam and diesel locomotives on the same weekend. One of the visitors for this event came in the form of DRS Class 37 diesel locomotive No. 37038, which is seen passing through Weybourne with a mixed freight train.

As well as No. 37038, they also had another visitor in the form of Class 42 Warship No. D832 *Onslaught* from the Ecclesbourne Valley Railway. D832 made light work of Kelling Bank with its powerful (yet noisy) hydraulic engine. This is only one of two Warships that have made it into preservation with the other classmate, No. D821 *Greyhound*, being the other example. D821 can be seen in the Great Central Railway chapter.

Before moving to the Mid Norfolk Railway, Class 47 diesel locomotive No. 47367 spent many years at the North Norfolk Railway. It was used during the railway's diesel gala event in a sweltering May 2012. It is seen departing in the usual Class 47 style from Weybourne with a service for Sheringham.

Visitors to the diesel gala in May 2012 were invited to try No. E79960 between Weybourne and Holt. It is a 1958 railcar built by Waggon und Maschinenbau and was originally going to be used as an economic way to operate services on little used branch lines in the UK. However this never materialised and it now resides on the North Norfolk Railway.

The North Norfolk Railway operates a small number of diesel multiple units on the line. Class 101s like No. M51192, seen at Holt, were at one point very common in East Anglia before being replaced with more modern units. Sporting a Network SouthEast Railway Society headboard, it awaits departure for Sheringham.

Seen sat at Holt after arriving with a service from Sheringham in June 2016, Class 31 No. D5631 is one of the railway's home fleet diesel locomotives. The appearance of this locomotive differs as it doesn't wear a yellow warning panel on the cab ends, which is a standard requirement for all trains working on the mainline. D5631 also spent a lot of its life in East Anglia, being allocated to Stratford depot at one point during its life. It has been given a new lease of life on the North Norfolk Railway.

Seen at the headshunt, at Holt, is No. 66772, which is on loan to the North Norfolk Railway from GBRf for their diesel gala in June 2016. This attracted many visitors due to the rarity of a locomotive such as this being seen in this area. It also wore a Network SouthEast headboard, despite the four-year gap between NSE finishing in 1994 and the first Class 66 arriving into the UK in 1998.

10

Convoys

When preserved railways announce their gala event line-ups, they sometimes have locos that can't travel on the UK network on their own. This is usually due to them needing main line certification and required an Automatic Warning System (AWS) and a Train Protection Warning System (TPWS), which are required for the signals on the UK rail network. This is because trains will run over a magnet on the track that activates the AWS system onboard the train with a ding noise, usually telling the driver that the signal is green or an alarm will go off if the signal shows an amber or red aspect. This requires action from the driver, otherwise an emergency brake application will occur. Should the train pass a red signal, the TPWS will activate and an emergency brake application will occur.

Most of the locos seen in these convoys had to be hauled to preserved railways as they are not allowed to operate on their own on the network.

Seen passing through Thetford station in June 2013, from the North Norfolk Railway, was a convoy led by Devon & Cornwall Railways Class 56 No. 56311. The locos being hauled by 56311 were Nos 45133, 33108, 56301 and D5613 (31190).

In June 2014 another North Norfolk Railway convoy was seen at Thetford, led this time by No. D407 (50007) *Hercules*. The convoy behind D407 consisted of Class 20 No. D8059, Class 40 No. D306 and No. 37219.

A convoy led by Devon & Cornwall Railways Class 31 No. D5613 (31190), from the Mid Norfolk Railway to the East Lancashire Railway in July 2013, resulted in this colourful mix, consisting of Nos 47367, 73210, 50026 and 47596 behind the leading loco.

In May 2012, Devon & Cornwall Railways Class 31s Nos 31601 and 31602 were allocated the task of hauling Nos 55019 and 47596 from the Mid-Norfolk Railway to the North Norfolk Railway for their diesel gala. The convoy is seen arriving into Wymondham before reversing into the Mid-Norfolk Railway. Unfortunately, all didn't go to plan as there was a paperwork issue with 47596, which meant it had to be transferred by road.

June 2016 saw this colourful convoy passing through Wymondham on its way to the North Norfolk Railway. Led and trailed by GBRf Class 66s Nos 66710 and 66772, the convoy consisted of Nos 50026 and 33035 and headed towards Norwich. 66772 was used for the gala but 66710 wasn't.

In March 2017, the Mid-Norfolk Railway took delivery of former DRS Class 37 diesel locomotive No. 37688, which was working alongside No. 37423, which was on its way from Willesden to Norwich Crown Point. It is seen passing Ely nearing journeys end onto the Breckland Line.

For the mixed traction event in June 2019, the North Norfolk Railway hired two visitors from DRS in the form of Nos 57002 and 57003. Sat in Norwich yard in the rain, this pair were late leaving due to No. 745104 failing to their left and fouling the points that allowed them to depart.